# Babysitting Grandpa

**written by**
**John R. Scannell**

**illustrated by**
**Devika Joglekar**

Wutherwood Press

For Missy, Mandy, Becky, and Ben

My four wonderful children

who provided years of excellent practice

for Grandpa.

I knew something was up when the doorbell rang. The doorbell never rings this early. Daddy Nick had already scooted off to catch his bus at the park-and-ride, and Mommy was dressed to go to work.

Mommy is a doctor. Some-day, when I get into a discussion about "What do your parents do?," I'll be miles ahead when I tell everyone that Mommy and Daddy are both college graduates—making me their little Cougar mascot, of course —and that Mommy is a family praktishuner.

(I probably spelled that wrong, but hey, I'm only a year old and I'm not used to spell-check yet.)

My Daddy is an IT specialist. That pleases me because Daddy Nick is definitely IT. Mommy Mandy feels the same way about him as I do.

Like I said, I knew something different was happening this morning because Mommy wasn't dashing around getting me ready to go to my daycare. I must proudly confess that I am already in college—well, the college daycare anyway—at Bellevue College. But today I wasn't going to daycare. Mommy and Daddy said today is Veterans Day.

I don't know what that means, but they told me that my great grandpa and some of my great uncles and one of my uncles are veterans, so it is a special day for them.

They also said that my Mommy's sister, Aunt Missy, was almost a veteran, but that she tore her knee ligament when she was in Rotsee at her Wazzu college, so she never became a soldier. I don't know what a Rotsee is, but I'm going to avoid it so my knees don't get hurt.

My Aunt Missy went to Wazzu just like Mommy and Daddy did.
A college named Wazzu. Isn't that a silly name? Mommy told me
Aunt Missy is a landscape architect who can do magic with trees
and flowers because she has a green thumb. Wow!

I looked for it when Aunt Missy was here on my birthday, but
I couldn't see it. Maybe only grown-ups can see certain things.

When the doorbell rang Mommy hollered, "Come on in," and in walked Grandpa. I'm pretty sure that's his name because Mommy said, "Good morning, Grandpa," and Mommy is never wrong. Then Mommy showed him where my food is—the squeeze fruit pouches that I love were on the counter and the yogurt was in the refrigerator. Mommy pointed to the bananas next to the fridge and told Grandpa that I could eat a whole banana if I wanted. A whole banana. Did I mention that I'm only one?

Then Mommy showed Grandpa where my diapers were, both upstairs and downstairs, and showed him where I sleep when it's time for my nap. Mommy showed Grandpa where I keep all my blocks and toys—I like spreading them out in the living room. As you probably know, toys need breathing space.

Then Mommy wrote down some things for Grandpa in a tiny notebook and said, "This is when Opal eats," and "This is when she'll probably take a nap." Grandpa nodded his head a lot and kept saying, "Okay." I think he works for Mommy, but I'm not sure. Grandpa just kept smiling at me—he did that a lot and made funny noises. Grandpa seemed happy to see me.

And then before I knew it, Mommy was gone. I heard the garage door close, and then I knew it was just me and Grandpa... oh, and Charlie, too. Charlie is my dog, and we take good care of one another.

Grandpa put me on the living room floor in the middle of my blocks. He and I played my favorite game, "Knock Down the Stack."

Grandpa would stack up a bunch of blocks, and I would knock them down. It's a good test to measure the patience of whomever is taking care of me.

Grandpa didn't seem to get tired of it, so I stood up and headed down the hallway toward the front door.

The "Heading for the Front Door" gambit is a test, too. I wanted to see how long it would take Grandpa to come after me. He was still stretched out among my blocks when I got within inches of the front door. He looked up, but he didn't seem concerned. "Hey, Peanut," he said, "where are you going?" I think he knew I couldn't reach the doorknob—I'm pretty short—but one of these days I'm going to surprise everyone when I actually reach up and make my dash out the door into the sunshine.

But today wasn't going to be that day. Grandpa hadn't even stirred. He'd called my bluff.

So I upped the ante by climbing up the bottom stair that leads upstairs. Let me tell you; that got his attention. Before I knew it, Grandpa was sitting on the second step and watching me struggle to get up to the landing. It was like he appeared out of nowhere. I made it all the way up, and then I turned around and sat down. Climbing stairs is hard work.

So what does Grandpa do? Does he applaud me saying, "Good job, Peanut?" I wish. He just picks me up and burbles my tummy. You know what that is, right? Someone puts their mouth against your tummy and vibrates their lips.

That tickled and it made me laugh. Grandpa burbled my tummy a lot that day. I think burbling is something that Grandpas like to do; I'm not sure.

After burbling, he put me down in the hallway. I immediately toddled over to the shoe bin—everyone takes off their shoes when they come into my house—and snatched up one of my pink sneakers which was sitting in the bin among Daddy's and Mommy's shoes.

I like carrying shoes around. My dog Charlie prefers socks, but me, I like shoes. Sometimes I empty the shoe bin for Mommy because I love it when she tells me how helpful I am. My helpfulness makes me especially cute.

I decided it was time to get back to my scattered blocks, but along the way, my attention was diverted by the paper-recycling bin that Mommy and Daddy keep next to the desk at the end of the hallway. This is one of my favorite spots. Blocks may be fun, but paper...well...it is difficult to say how much fun I have with paper.

It crinkles. It bends. It rips. It scatters. And after Charlie has it in his mouth, it's sticky. Sticky paper is the best.

I hope I am not revealing a trade secret here, but Charlie and I are confederates. He is my playmate, and he loves paper as much as I do. Probably more.
(I hope nothing I say gets Charlie in trouble.)

Typically, when no one is looking, I go into the paper-recycling bin next to the desk and pull out a piece of cardboard or an envelope. Usually a couple of pieces at a time. Charlie is right behind me waiting for the hand-off, kind of like a Seattle Seahawks running back.

Charlie takes the piece of paper from me and heads to the front room where he can have a leisurely chew. He's much better at tearing up paper than I am. When I get better at it, Charlie and I can have a contest.

Grandpa caught onto to the game of "Take the Paper and Run" pretty quickly. C'est dommage. (That's French for, "It's a pity." Becoming bilingual is just one of the advantages of going to daycare at an accredited college.)

But here's the thing. Grandpa went into the front room to get the paper from Charlie who had managed to tear it up pretty well in no time at all. While Grandpa was picking up all the damp, dog-slobbered pieces, I headed to Charlie's water bowl near the back door. Paper chewing may be fun, but splashing water out of Charlie's water bowl—well, does it get any better than that?

"Okay, Opal," Grandpa said, as I splashed and giggled, "I think it is time for breakfast."

He swept me up and got me belted into my highchair. He was singing something like "Let's eat breakfast, my fair lady," when he unscrewed the top of my apple-peach-flavored fruit tube. He gave the tube a good squeeze, and I reached out to take it from him. I may only be one-year-old, but I have really smart parents, and I'm in a collegiate daycare. I can feed myself.

Grandpa gave me two fruit tubes. I can tell he's an easy touch. When I was feeding envelopes to Charlie or splashing around in Charlie's water bowl, he never raised his voice. He laughed. When he laughed, I laughed, too. Grandpa is a good audience.

Perhaps I should not discuss what happened next. You can probably guess. Let me put this as delicately as I can. When you put something in one end, it is likely to come out the other... right? Every human is subject to the same biological imperatives. My Mommy, who is a doctor, says poop is an imperative.

Fortunately, it didn't seem to bother Grandpa, and he whisked me upstairs and changed me. I suspect he's done this before. I look forward to the day when I can change my own diapers—but now I must rely on the kindness of Mommy and Daddy and... a man named Grandpa.

We went back downstairs, and Charlie and I reprised our morning antics. It was another round of "Take the Paper and Run" and "Climb the Stairs."

I added a new game, too. "Clear the Bookshelf." Mommy and Daddy have a bookcase in the front room, and they keep a lot of books tucked away—so many books that I can't see the back of the bookcase.

I love the look of wood—and I prefer an unobstructed view—that's why I always clear the books off the shelf.

Grandpa doesn't understand my aesthetic sensibilities any more than Mommy and Daddy do, because he picked me up, burbled my belly, and immediately began reshelving the books. Apparently adults would rather look at the backs of the books than the back of the bookshelf.

Somehow, I managed to clear my own bookshelf that holds my special books. Grandpa didn't feel obliged to reshelve those books until minutes before Mommy came home.

That's pretty much how the morning went. Grandpa would usually be a few feet away, or sometimes he would be lying down amidst my blocks and laughing at me.

He also kept sitting on our comfy blue sofa and writing notes. I'm not sure what he was writing, but he seemed to be having a good time, so I let him write.

He doesn't seem like a tattle-tale to me—or a spy.

Before I knew it, lunch was being served. I had two tubs of strawberry-vanilla yogurt, and I let Grandpa feed me so he could feel useful. Adults are like that. You have to give them something to do or they get unhappy. I realize that for the time being, my job is to give adults something to do. I serve a very useful purpose in the lives of Mommy and Daddy—and now, Grandpa, too. Grandpa liked to play "Airplane" with spoonsful of yogurt, and I dutifully played along, enjoying each mouthful as the yummy yogurt came in for a smooth landing on my tongue.

As you may know, I taste a lot of things during the course of the day. Blocks, book edges, cardboard, and paper. Earlier that morning, I was tasting Mommy and Daddy's shoes, and I gotta say, yogurt has shoes beat all to heck.

Grandpa had no sooner wiped my hands and face—as you know, yogurt smears really well—when I felt a post-lunch malaise creeping over me. I yawned, and Grandpa took that as a signal to take me upstairs to my dimly-lit nursery. Grandpa changed me, found a new pair of warm slacks for me, and then lay me down in the crib, covering me with a fuzzy blanket with really smooth edges. He also gave me my binky which is, as everyone acknowledges, a premier sleep aid.

You ever have one of those moments when you are sleepy until someone puts you in your crib? Well, this was one of those moments. Fortunately, Grandpa had the cure: Goldilocks and the Three Bears. He said it was an old fairy tale by Robert Southey, but I had my suspicions when he started:

Once upon a time there were three bears who lived in federally-subsidized housing in the middle of a large, heavily-wooded national park somewhere in northwestern Wyoming. The father's name was Smokey and his son was Little Smoke. Mama Bear was Smoke-Free...always a good thing...

I worry that Grandpa changes stories without giving proper attribution to the original author. I didn't ask him if Mr. Southey would like Grandpa's version. That, however, is something for another day. And I might have brought up Grandpa's plagiarism, but I fell asleep.

Grandpa's stories—even if they are plagiarized, borrowed, or completely derivative—are really terrific for putting me to sleep. Grandma Wendy says that's true even for her. She says that Grandpa's stories are the most terrific soporific. (I'm gonna have to look up soporific before I graduate from pre-school.)

Anyway, I fell asleep. Grandpa says I fell asleep for two hours, and that may be true. I don't yet have any real sense of time. When I'm sleepy, I sleep. When I'm hungry, I eat. When I woke up, it was time to eat. Oh, yes!

Grandpa had pulled out a box of crackers, and he handed them to me one-by-one so I could snack while playing blocks. My good friend, Charlie, vacuumed the floor while I ate the crackers.

Grandpa mistakenly seemed to think that crackers would fill the bill for snack time, so I had to put him straight. I toddled over to my highchair and grabbed its footrest and turned and looked at him over my shoulder. Fortunately, Grandpa is a quick study. He strapped me into my highchair for an afternoon banana.

I ate the whole thing. By myself. I don't wanna brag, but hey, did I mention I'm only one-year-old?

So it was back to playing with blocks, handing Charlie some envelopes—you know the drill. My days are busy, busy, busy.

Before I knew it, Mommy was home, and she and Grandpa laughed a lot and pointed to me when they laughed.

I'm glad I could make them laugh. Making adults smile is hard work, but someone has to do it.

Grandpa gave me a smooch and a smile, hugged my Mommy, said, "I love you, Peanut," and then he was out the door. I think he likes working for Mommy.

I think I took pretty good care of him today.

# Postscript

Yep. I think I took pretty good care of Grandpa that day, and I was only one-year-old! A year later, Mommy and Daddy gave me a brand new brother, Walter, as a reward. I expect Grandpa will come over again soon, and when he does, I'm going to let Walter babysit him—a Grandpa can be hard work.

CPSIA information can be obtained
at www.ICGtesting.com
Printed in the USA
BVHW020512040121
596798BV00002B/8